DINOSAUR HUNT

DINOSAUR HUNT

GEORGE O. WHITAKER

WITH

JOAN MEYERS

ILLUSTRATED WITH PHOTOGRAPHS BY GEORGE O. WHITAKER
CHIEF PREPARATOR AND HEAD OF THE LABORATORY OF THE
DEPARTMENT OF VERTEBRATE PALEONTOLOGY AT THE
AMERICAN MUSEUM OF NATURAL HISTORY IN NEW YORK CITY

AND LINE DRAWINGS BY MICHAEL INSINNA, STAFF ARTIST AT
THE AMERICAN MUSEUM OF NATURAL HISTORY

HARCOURT, BRACE & WORLD, INC., NEW YORK

DINOSAUR HUNT

1

On a sunny day late in the spring of 1947, two men drove toward Albuquerque, New Mexico. They were coming down from Lindrith, a small town in the northern section of the state.

For the first lap of their journey, from Lindrith to Cuba, they traveled over a dirt road. They were in fine spirits, and part of their good humor came from the fact that the surface of this road was dry. After a heavy rain in New Mexico, many of the back roads become almost impassable. Even jeeps such as the one George Whitaker and Bill Fish were driving — supposed to go anywhere with their four-wheel drive — would skid on the slick surface and bog down in the mudholes. Then it might take twelve hours to drive the thirty miles from Lindrith to Cuba.

Today, however, they were lucky. They had only the dust to cope with, and not too much of that unless another car passed them. Forty-five minutes after leaving Lindrith, they hit a paved highway, New Mexico 44, just outside of Cuba. (See the map on

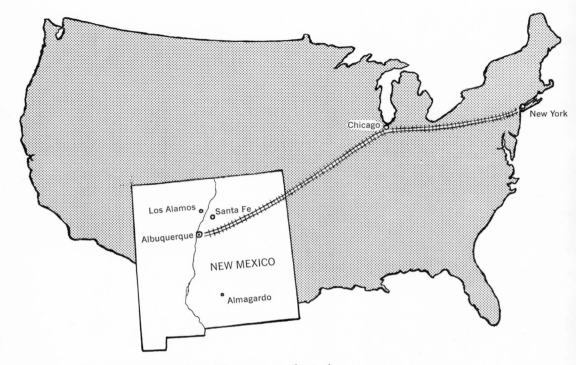

From New York to Albuquerque, by train

page 20.) That state highway would take them into Albuquerque, some ninety miles away.

The scenery was spectacular. Fantastic cliffs loomed above arid, barren flatlands. Looking down as the jeep topped a rise, the two men could see the highway extending for miles in front of them. It seemed to end only where earth met sky far off in the distance. At the horizon, the color of the sky softened, but overhead it was a brilliant blue, and the sun shone with searing intensity. The depths of space around them, both of earth and sky, seemed infinite and ageless. It was hard to imagine man in this enormous landscape and easy to imagine that monster creatures — dinosaurs — had roamed here millions of years ago.

These men were dinosaur hunters. They belonged to the staff of the American Museum of Natural History in New York City, one of the most famous museums in the world. George and Bill were not chasing live dinosaurs. The last one had died some sixty to seventy million years ago. They were hunting fossil remains.

When the word "fossil" was coined in the sixteenth century from the Latin *fossilis*, meaning "dug up," it referred to any curious object found buried. Nowadays, a fossil is defined as any remains or trace (such as a skeleton, footprint, or perhaps even simply the impress of a leaf) of an animal or plant that is extinct. And when something is called extinct, it means that the last one of its kind is dead. Usually, fossils are from former ages of the earth. (You will find a geologic timetable on page 11 of this book.) This story is about an extinct animal that George Whitaker found.

As a small boy, George had been fascinated by bones of all kinds. He lived in a small town in Georgia and kept the skeletons of cows and horses — when he could get hold of them — in his bedroom. These are not extinct animals, so their bones do not qualify as fossils, but as he grew up, George became interested in fossil bones as well.

After he got out of the Army, he decided to work with fossils for the rest of his life. He came to the American Museum of Natural History in New York to apply for a job and was sent by a guard to Dr. George Gaylord Simpson, a paleontologist on the Museum staff.

A paleontologist is a particular kind of scientist. He is a person who studies fossils in order to understand why and how animals or plants have changed over great periods of time — the operation of the "general law" of evolution.

Unfortunately, Dr. Simpson had to tell George Whitaker that there were no jobs available at the Museum. George begged to be allowed to work in the laboratory, even if it meant going without pay. Because Dr. Simpson felt that anyone with that strong an interest ought to be given a chance, he arranged for George to work on a volunteer basis at the Museum. After a few months, he was put on the payroll and became a permanent member of the staff.

This is an unusual way to go about getting a job, but it worked out very well for George. During the years that followed, he traveled to many parts of the world, frequently with Dr. Simpson, collecting fossils and dreaming about making unusual finds.

Summers are the paleontologists' seasons in the field, and this is the story of how, that summer in New Mexico, George Whitaker did make an important discovery. He found the *Coelophysis* (Seel-o-fy'-sis), a little dinosaur that was a predecessor of bigger and better known North American dinosaurs. This is also the story of how his find was brought back safely to New York City and put on exhibit in the Dinosaur Hall at the Museum.

That spring day in 1947 might be called the beginning of this adventure, for although George and Bill had been in New Mexico for a few weeks already, their time had been spent picking up the jeeps and camping gear, collecting equipment that they had stored in New Mexico during the past winter, and setting up camp at Lindrith.

On June 10, they left for Albuquerque, where they were to pick up the rest of the summer's field party. Dr. Simpson was

The history of the earth ⟶

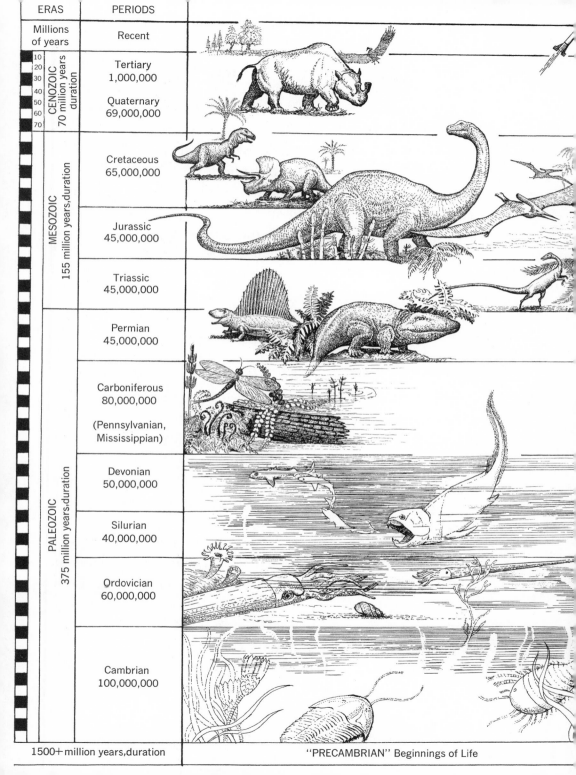

ERAS	PERIODS
Millions of years	**Recent**
CENOZOIC 70 million years duration	**Tertiary** 1,000,000
	Quaternary 69,000,000
MESOZOIC 155 million years, duration	**Cretaceous** 65,000,000
	Jurassic 45,000,000
	Triassic 45,000,000
PALEOZOIC 375 million years, duration	**Permian** 45,000,000
	Carboniferous 80,000,000 (Pennsylvanian, Mississippian)
	Devonian 50,000,000
	Silurian 40,000,000
	Ordovician 60,000,000
	Cambrian 100,000,000

1500+ million years, duration   "PRECAMBRIAN" Beginnings of Life

coming, as well as another paleontologist, Dr. Edwin H. Colbert. The third man was a friend of Dr. Colbert's, Dr. Thomas Ierardi. He was a division director of physical education at City College in New York City and was planning to spend the summer sketching in the Southwest. He had agreed to help with chores. The men from the Museum came out under funds provided for in the Museum budget or by gifts from so-called "angels," wealthy people who were interested in financing specific expeditions. Thomas Ierardi took care of his own expenses.

As George and Bill drove along, they looked as if they had spent all their lives in the Southwest. Both men were tanned and muscular from doing hard work in the open air. George was particularly fond of the way the local people dressed, and along with his khaki trousers and work shirt, he wore a cowboy hat and a turquoise-and-silver bracelet. In the Southwest, it is not unusual for men to wear this sort of jewelry. The bracelet had been made by a Navajo Indian and pawned at the New Mexican trading post where George had found it.

Piñon and juniper trees, their branches distorted by the dryness of the climate and flattened by the constant wind, grew over the cliffs along the sides of the highway. Small cholla cactus grew in the fields, and there were acres of gray-green sage, an almost inedible plant not even useful for its fiber.

Nowadays, there is almost no water in the Southwest, but once upon a time, the sea ran through there, laying down sediment deposits — silt and sandstone. Reptiles swarmed there then. Eventually the sea began to retreat; the earth warped upward, and wind and water erosion carved the cliffs into the fantastic shapes they still retain. As the sea retreated and came in again, the di-

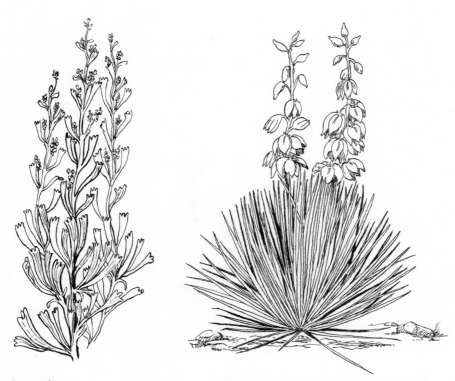

Sage plant   *Yucca, the state flower of New Mexico*

nosaurs grew heavier and more grotesque. At last, the sea made a final retreat, the dinosaurs disappeared forever from the scene, and one of the most dramatic chapters in earth's history was closed.

No one knows exactly why this is so. Dr. Simpson, in his book called *Life of the Past*, wrote that although many people have thought of possible causes, the record is not complete enough to say which were actually involved. "All we can say at present is that something changed and dinosaurs did not. What changed and why the dinosaurs failed to cope with the change are among the things still hidden from us."

But the big reptiles left behind a permanent record. Under the pickaxes of the fossil hunters, their bones reappear millions of years later, at a time when the only sea left in the Southwest is that of sage.

Cholla cactus

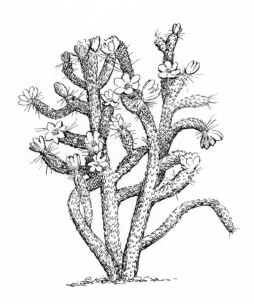

2

It was sweltering hot in Albuquerque that day. George remembers it as being above 100° Fahrenheit at the railroad station.

When they met, Dr. Simpson and Dr. Colbert were eager to find out from George and Bill how the first work had been going. They were all glad to see each other. They were glad, too, to get out of the city and onto the highway, where the speeding jeep created a breeze of its own.

They had to climb to get back to Lindrith, which was about 6,600 feet above sea level, while Albuquerque was only 4,950 feet. It is supposed to get cooler the higher up you go, the temperature dropping on an average of $3\frac{1}{2}°$ F. for every 1,000 feet. But to say that something happens "on an average" is to say that it doesn't necessarily work that way all the time. There are other things that affect temperature besides just height. For one thing, the air cools off after the sun goes down. In camp at Lindrith one night, the thermometer dropped to about 20° F. George still remembers Dr. Colbert chopping ice out of his washbasin

Leaving Albuquerque for Lindrith. Dr. Simpson (left) and Dr. Colbert (right) are in the front jeep.

the next morning. Although extremes in temperature are not rare in the Southwest, this much of a variation was rather unusual.

In camp, the first day was spent in orienting themselves, going over maps of the area and field notes, and arranging to split up the party. Two separate expeditions had been planned.

16

Since George and Bill had already found some bones at the Lindrith camp, the fossil remains of a mammal called *Meniscotherium* (Me-nis'-ko-the'-ri-um), Dr. Simpson was going to stay there and work with Bill Fish.

Both Dr. Simpson and Dr. Colbert were paleontologists, but they had different specialties. Dr. Simpson's was the life of mammals in past geological periods. All animals that nourish their young with milk are called mammals. Mammals belong to the highest class of vertebrates, or animals with backbones.

Dr. Colbert's specialty was reptiles — a class of air-breathing animals with backbones (also vertebrates, therefore, but of a lower order than mammals). Alligators and crocodiles are reptiles, as are lizards, snakes, turtles, and other animals, such as dinosaurs, that have become extinct.

Dr. Colbert was particularly interested in the first dinosaurs. He wondered how they had evolved — that is, how they had come into being and grown and changed the way they did.

Scientists nowadays believe that all animals or plants come from other kinds that were there before them, even though sometimes they don't look at all the same. Most of the time, each generation is slightly different in some way — the changes are gradual.

Dinosaurs originated in the Triassic Period, roughly 200 million years ago. Although fossil remains of Triassic dinosaurs have been found scattered all over the world — in the Connecticut Valley, in Germany, South Africa, China, and Brazil — they are still rare and not much is known about them.

The existence of one little ancestral dinosaur from the Triassic

17

was discovered back in the 1880's by one of the great field men in the history of paleontology. David Baldwin, while prospecting in New Mexico, had turned up a few scraps (approximately a small teacupful) of bone.

He sent them to Dr. Edward Drinker Cope, a member of the Academy of Natural Sciences in Philadelphia. Dr. Cope described these bones in 1887 and applied the name *Coelophysis* to them in 1889.

Triangles indicate localities where Triassic dinosaurs have been found.

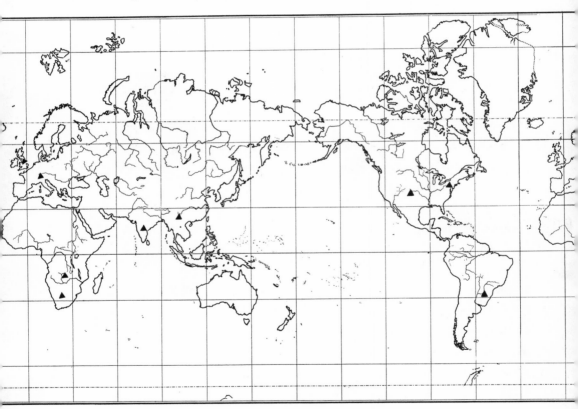

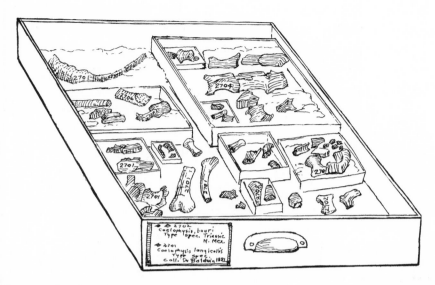

Tray at the American Museum of Natural History containing the Coelophysis *bone found by Baldwin*

In the notes that David Baldwin sent Dr. Cope, he described the spot where he picked these bones up as being "against the variegated cliffs on the Rio Salino creek about eight miles north of Abiquiu." As you can see from the map on page 20, Abiquiu is not far from Lindrith. Dr. Colbert had no real hope that his expedition would be so lucky as to turn up more *Coelophysis* bone — no one ever had since David Baldwin — but he wanted to look around in the New Mexico Triassic strata.

He had a colleague, Professor C. L. Camp of the University of California, who for many years had been one of the leading explorers of the Triassic in New Mexico. Dr. Camp had collected quite a lot of *phytosaur* (fy'-tow-sar) bone in New Mexico. Phytosaurs are early Triassic reptiles but not dinosaurs.

It is customary, when someone is already working in a particular area, that no one else goes there to collect. Paleontologists consider this part of their code of ethics. But Dr. Camp had already decided not to do any more work in New Mexico. He knew of Dr. Colbert's interests and had sent him his "locality data." Some of it was from a place called Ghost Ranch, located where David Baldwin had made his find. Dr. Colbert planned, therefore, to work in the Triassic of the Southwest, at Ghost Ranch and other places.

Detail map, northwest corner of New Mexico

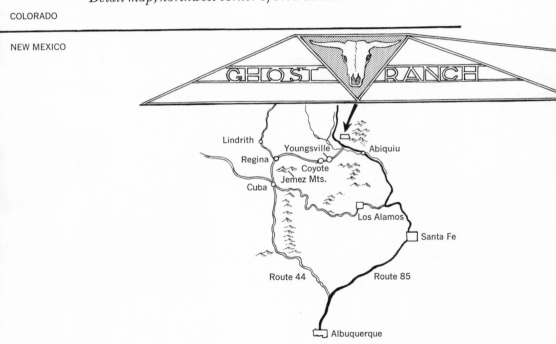

Entrance to Ghost Ranch

The second morning in camp, the group at Lindrith decided they would make a "windshield" survey. They piled into the jeeps and drove around the Jemez (Hay'-mes) mountain range, which you can see on the map on page 20. Dr. Simpson and Bill Fish went along. Although they knew where *they* were going to be working, they were curious to see what spot their colleagues would pick.

Over by Coyote, they saw some beautiful variegated cliffs (see pages 22 and 23) in which the different geologic ages were clearly defined in the exposed rock formation. These magnificent cliffs were on Ghost Ranch property. Soon after, they passed a sign with the skull of a steer painted on it. It was the work of Georgia O'Keeffe, a famous American artist who lived in the Southwest

21

for many years. Her paintings frequently emphasize the beauty of the curving lines of bones. Professor Camp had mentioned that sign. The men drove past it, on to the main house, to talk to Arthur Pack, the owner of Ghost Ranch.

Cliff formation at Ghost Ranch

Most landowners are cooperative with scientists who want to work on their property, though they tend to find it all a bit peculiar. Only once did George have trouble in getting a landowner's permission. This was near the Petrified Forest in Arizona, where there was a fine specimen within sight of the road, but on the other side of a fence. There was a gate in the fence, and George tried to get the owner of the land to let him go through the gate.

"No," the owner said, "that gate's locked and it stays locked."

"Well," George said, "if you would show us how, we could lock it up again after ourselves. Or maybe we could come and get you every time we want to go in or out."

The answer was still no. "If people see tracks going in, then they'll want to come in and out, too. But I'll tell you what I'll do," the owner said. "You can collect the specimen if you want to, but you have to go in the back way."

And that is what George finally did. He drove fifty miles each way, through back woods, to get to a location that was within sight of the road!

Mr. Pack, however, proved to be more than cooperative. Ghost Ranch was one of the larger ranches in New Mexico, being at that time over 50,000 acres. Arthur Pack and his wife had run it as a dude ranch for about ten years until World War II came along; Mr. Pack had always enjoyed having lots of people around. He not only gave his enthusiastic permission for any digging the fossil collectors might care to do on his property; he also gave them a campsite by his swimming pool. This was an unusual piece of luck, considering how hot it gets in New Mexico during the summer. It was, in fact, the only time in George's entire fossil-hunting career that he *ever* camped by a swimming pool.

Swimming pool at Ghost Ranch. Carl Sorensen is at the left and George Whitaker at the right.

Looking down on Ghost Ranch

3

Where do fossil hunters usually camp? Nowadays, because of jeeps or other kinds of powered vehicles, they can pitch their tents a few miles away from where they intend to work and still not waste too much time getting back and forth. This was the situation at Ghost Ranch. But back in the nineteenth century, David Baldwin — alone in wild country except for his burro — would bed himself down at night wherever he happened to be. Cars hadn't yet been invented.

Baldwin had other problems that modern expeditions aren't bothered by. For one thing, sometimes he found more fossils than his burro could carry. Then he would have to stash them away and make a note of the location. Later on he would come back to pick them up and ship them off to various collectors. Nowadays, a jeep will carry more bones than any burro could, inside or outside.

The heat becomes almost unbearable in the badlands during the summer months, and Baldwin couldn't carry enough water with him to survive. By doing his collecting during the winter instead, when snow lay on the northern slopes of the hills, he could stay out for months at a time. Nowadays, expeditions go out during the summer months because they can haul water for themselves over long distances.

Modern fossil hunters work as hard as they can during the long daylight hours of the summer. A field season usually lasts only ninety or one hundred days. A museum has a limited supply of money to spend on collecting in the field, and the men are needed back at the museum the rest of the time, anyway.

A typical day in the field begins with the alarm clock going off at about a quarter to five in the morning, when it is still dark. The campers roll off their cots or climb out of their sleeping bags. One of the men starts the gas-burning Coleman stove, and soon they are eating pancakes and drinking black coffee.

Off they go to work, taking plenty of water with them. At noon, they pause to eat the sandwiches they have brought along and then resume work until the sun goes down — perhaps about six-thirty or seven in the evening. Sometimes, during the afternoon, one of the men will take a jeep and drive into the nearest town or trading post for supplies. By sinking a block of ice with sawdust around it into the ground at camp, they can keep meat fresh for two or three days. Most of their meals are very simple. When they get back to camp in the evenings, usually the men are too tired to fuss with anything — which is one of the reasons they use a gas stove instead of building a campfire. They have to write up their field notes in the evenings, as well.

Fossil hunters have to forget about getting to work at nine o'clock and going home at five or about taking time out for

Dr. Colbert and Tom Ierardi carrying supplies to the Ghost Ranch quarry

Sundays and holidays. They are not paid for the overtime they put in. One of their standard jokes is that they have to get special permission from the museum to work as hard as they do.

Fossil hunting is no job for weaklings; it takes a lot of stamina to work carefully in the hot sun day after day. Other aspects of the weather can be disagreeable, too: small whirlwinds skitter across fossil country; sometimes a sudden sandstorm blows up; or a cloudburst can engulf the fossil hunters in a downpour.

28

Pesty pack rats get into their camp supplies at night. And, too, rattlesnakes are a constant danger in this country.

Collections are acquired for museums by dedicated people who enjoy what they are doing in spite of the hardships attached to their work.

George Whitaker in camp

4

George, Tom Ierardi, and Dr. Colbert moved from Lindrith over to Ghost Ranch on a Wednesday. They set up their tents in the morning and, in the afternoon, headed for the cliffs. Here they would begin prospecting.

The rocks in the badland areas of the Southwest have eroded over the years into fantastic and intricate shapes. Although these badlands, which are inhospitable to most living things, plant or animal, get very little rain, sudden downpours and wind have worn away most of the topsoil, exposing once-buried bone, which makes the Southwest an ideal place to hunt for fossils.

An expert can "walk out" an area very quickly, looking for contrasting colors and shapes. Sometimes scraps of bone can be found lying on the surface of the ground. Fossil hunters never begin digging without finding enough exposed material to be sure their work will turn up something.

Most surface scraps, or "float," are weathered-out, isolated pieces. It takes a trained eye to determine whether digging is

30

likely to produce more of the specimen. Most often the answer is no. But a piece of bone that looks freshly broken is worth going in after. A paleontologist might use a crooked awl or a Marsh pick to do a rough job of scraping off the surface. If he doesn't turn up the rest of the bone pretty quickly, he probably will give up and go on. Chances are it's just not there.

Whether the surface scraps are valuable depends upon what they are. For instance, usually a piece of rib is not worth keeping. Neither are broken pieces of turtle shell or fish scales. It is up to the collector to decide whether what he has found has enough character to be usable. This ability is acquired only by

The area the field party set out to prospect at Ghost Ranch

experience. A small piece may look completely worthless, but some small pieces have helped fill in large gaps in our knowledge about life on this planet.

It is hard to plan work ahead, as a collector never can tell what his prospecting will turn up. On that first Wednesday afternoon, George found a phytosaur skull right away, and they spent the rest of the week taking it out. On Sunday, June 16, Dr. Colbert decided they would do half a day's prospecting and call it quits. As they left camp in the jeep, he said jokingly, "Now remember — the better the day, the better the deed!"

The sun was very bright; there were no clouds in the sky. George laughed and said, "Yes, I'll find something good today."

5

Dr. Colbert and Tom Ierardi started off in one direction and
George in another. George crossed the top of a ridge, looking for
fragments of bone. When he didn't find any, he dropped down
the hill and continued to look. At the very bottom, he found a
few loose scraps of bone lying on top of the sand. Because they
were random — that is, not in any particular order — and because he couldn't find any bone imbedded in the earth at that
spot, he decided that rains must have washed these scraps down
the slope.

He went back up, finding more pieces of fossil bone along the
way. This trail led him about halfway up the hill, where he found
a little ledge of bone exposed. He was excited, but he didn't yet
know how remarkable this find was going to turn out to be.

He looked again at the fragments he had picked up. It is not
easy to tell from a little bit of bone just what kind of animal it
used to be part of, but these scraps didn't look like the phytosaurs
they had been collecting. He wrapped the tiny pieces in the soft-

33

est material available, which happened to be his undershirt, so that he could carry them back safely to the jeep.

Since this was unfamiliar territory, he looked around carefully and put up a rock monument, such as Indians use, to mark the site so that he would know the exact spot when he came back.

George was sitting in the jeep when Tom Ierardi and Dr. Colbert got back about lunchtime. When George took the fossils out of his pocket and carefully unwrapped them, Dr. Colbert was full of excitement. He wanted to go back before lunch to see the site for himself.

Later Dr. Colbert wrote in *Natural History* magazine:

"As I looked at it, I felt the excitement that comes to one who glimpses treasures in the earth. For years we had hoped to find traces of these primitive little dinosaurs, and the features shown by these fossils could not be mistaken. The bones were small and delicate, and they were hollow. And

The scene a few minutes after George finds the Coelophysis. *You can trace his route by following the footprints.*

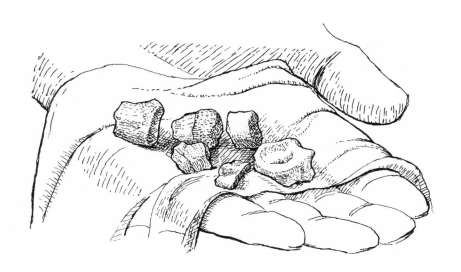

George holds the fragments he has found.

the little pieces of claw, by reason of its size and compressed shape, could have belonged to no other animal."

David Baldwin, back in the 1880's, must, like George, have found his scraps at the bottom of the slope. He, too, must have wondered whether they hadn't washed down from above. He surely tried to trace the material to its source, but obviously he had been unable to find further exposed bone — perhaps that little ledge of bone had still been covered over by red clay.

Fossil collecting is a hazardous business — neither Baldwin nor later Dr. Cope, when he came through the area after Baldwin had found the original fragments, went on to make the great discovery. But ever since then, fossil hunters had dreamed of turning up a complete skeleton.

It is rare, however, for the complete skeleton of any dinosaur to turn up. Dr. George Gaylord Simpson has estimated that more than 99 per cent of fossil dinosaurs found are represented only by fragments. ". . . the popular impression to the contrary notwithstanding, paleontologists cannot correctly restore missing parts of ancient animals unless the parts are known in closely related forms." He also remarks in his book, *Life of the Past*, that in very few of the extinct species is it known what all of their hard parts looked like.

The next question for George and Dr. Colbert was just what was in that ledge?

Dr. Colbert and Tom Ierardi on the spot

6

When someone is excited about something, it is hard not to rush ahead, but all good scientists have patience. George and Dr. Colbert knew that the quarry — the ledge — must be opened up carefully. Fossils can be very fragile.

Their hopes high, the three men set to work in good spirits to explore the small ledge. Tom Ierardi had become so interested in what was going on that he had put aside his sketching and was now working full time with Dr. Colbert and George. They began to remove the earth covering the bones. Each step of the way, accurate records had to be kept for the find to be of real scientific value.

Some of the first bones were easily recognizable as phytosaurs, and while the fossil hunters were not displeased at this, it wasn't very exciting and not at all what they had hoped to find. But as they went on, it became apparent that other bones were too small to be those of phytosaurs.

"Well, maybe they are babies . . ." George half joked.

The first bones are exposed on the slope.

Each time George and Tom Ierardi cleared a new small area, they would call Dr. Colbert over to have a look at what they had exposed.

"Well," Dr. Colbert would say, "this looks exactly like the leg bone of a small dinosaur, but it's just not . . ."

"Not what?" George asked.

And Dr. Colbert shook his head. Were they really finding all these things? "It's just too good," he said. "Look, here are ribs — and here vertebrae . . ."

They kept clearing the earth away, using picks and smaller tools, until they had uncovered a band of bone extending over an area of about twenty to thirty feet along the face of the cliff. Any place they dug in, they would find the same little bones.

They worked like this for about two weeks. Then one day, Tom Ierardi picked up what appeared to him to be hunk of rock. He looked at it and then asked Dr. Colbert to have a look at it.

If Dr. Colbert had had doubts before, he had them no longer. This was no phytosaur — it was unmistakably a primitive dinosaur. Tom Ierardi had picked up the front half of a skull with a jaw attached — the easiest parts of an animal to identify.

Part of the Coelophysis *skull, with jaw attached*

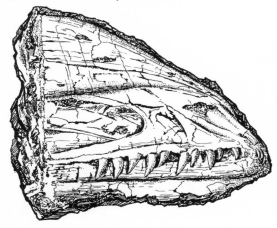

About this time they began to realize how long it was going to take them to get everything they wanted out of this quarry. Additional help would be needed. Dr. Colbert placed a call to the Museum back in New York, asking Carl Sorensen of the Vertebrate Paleontology Laboratory to come out and give them a hand.

Eventually, in the course of the two summers they worked there, they were to find literally dozens of complete skeletons

The proportions of a bone enable scientists to identify the particular kind of animal it came from. Some differences in these proportions are illustrated below, using six dorsal vertebrae from prehistoric animals and the dorsal vertebrae of a modern crocodile.

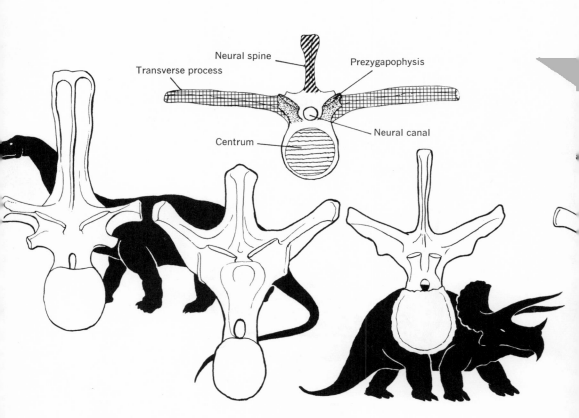

in the quarry, of all sizes, from babies to adults. Some day, perhaps scientists will know why so many of these little animals were herded together in this one deposit. The best guess is that some kind of accident happened — perhaps a dust storm came up or a sudden flood occurred; the bank of a stream might have caved in or the little dinosaurs might have been caught in a mudhole. It was apparent from the bentonite bands — a form of volcanic ash — in the silt with the bones that once there had been volcanic activity at that spot. Perhaps the little dinosaurs had gotten caught in a pocket of volcanic gases. Or possibly, the herd had come down to drink at a small pool that was poisonous. In any case, however they died, the dinosaurs had been completely covered — and thus preserved — before any of their bones could be dispersed.

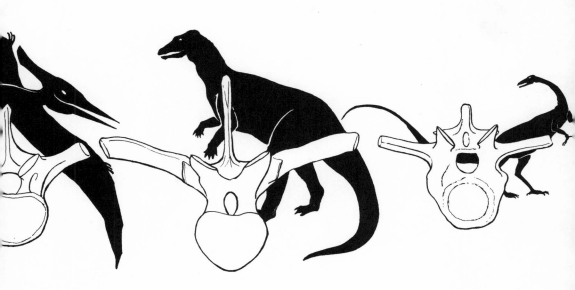

The details of such a find take years and years to work out. A great many factors have to be studied. Usually, the newspapers are most interested in fossils when they are first found, but scientists seldom know then exactly how important a find is going to be. In paleontology, as in few other subjects, a good deal of time usually elapses between a discovery and the realization of its proper meaning.

7

This was a tremendous find, and it caused quite a stir in the newspapers. There had been very few finds quite like it in the history of paleontology. The fossil hunters saw that they were going to be working at Ghost Ranch for a long time.

When Arthur Pack realized this, he told them to move into one of the houses on his ranch, an attractive adobe structure, quite typical of the buildings in that section of the country.

The house was about a mile from the hill where they were digging, and that mile had to be walked, because even a jeep could not cover the rough terrain between. Mr. Pack decided there was just too much work for the expedition at the quarry; they should not have to walk back and forth. He told his foreman, Herman Hall, to bulldoze a road so that a jeep might drive up to the bottom of the hill.

It took the foreman two days to make the road, and the fossil hunters were flabbergasted at their luck.

Working on the slope was quite difficult because of its steep

43

New headquarters for the Museum field party

Tom Ierardi and George Whitaker plastering the face of the ledge

angle. The men were afraid they might ruin some specimens if they dug their feet into the ground to help themselves stay on the hillside. George wished they had sky hooks to hang onto!

And there was another difficulty. A tremendous amount of rock, called over-burden, had built up on top of the fossils through the years. Now that rock had to be removed. First, the men laid down plaster of Paris to protect the part of the fossil bed already stripped to bone level. Then they attacked the over-burden with picks and shovels. Using these crude tools, they had to be certain to stop at least a foot above the bone. Otherwise, they were likely to do some damage to the fossils buried underneath.

Where they took out the rock, they built in a wooden platform some six feet above the buried fossils, high enough to allow headroom. The platform extended out about five feet and ran along the face of the cliff for almost thirty feet. It provided the fossil hunters with shade — very important in that country — and also acted as an umbrella, protecting both fossils and workers from being washed away by the occasional rain. Also, clay and rubble from higher up on the hill would be caught by this platform, instead of rolling down over the cleared area.

Now the remaining matrix — the term used for the material in which fossils are imbedded — had to be stripped down to the level of the bone. Matrix can be sandstone, limestone, loose sand, hardened mud, or clay; peat or coal; soil or river-bed gravel; or anything else that happens to surround fossils. Fossils are rarely or never found in some kinds of rock, but often in others. In this case, the bones of the *Coelophysis* were imbedded in a

Building the platform. Left to right: Carl Sorensen, George Whitaker, and Tom Ierardi

very fine-grained reddish silt stone with deposits of bentonite in it, called the Chinle formation.

Stripping this close to the bone must be done very delicately, using a large selection of special tools. (See the illustration on pages 48 and 49.) Small picks are used to free the matrix, and the surface is kept clean by brushing loose material away with whisk brooms or very fine camel's-hair brushes. Gradually, as it is un-

46

covered, the shape of a bone can be made out.

Instead of freeing each piece of bone right there in the quarry, they planned to remove large blocks of matrix containing the fossils. These would be sent to New York, where the matrix would be stripped away carefully from the bones. The problem was where to cut out these blocks. First, the men had to take off enough of the surface to see what they had. The best thing to have done next would have been to cut channels where the bone petered out, but that wasn't possible at Ghost Ranch. There, the skeletons were articulated, or completely joined together, lying on top of each other over an area of about six by thirty feet. Obviously, no block that big could be taken out.

The next best thing was to cut where the least possible amount of bone would have to be removed. But some parts of a skeleton — skulls or pelvic bones, for instance — might have more value than other parts to the scientists who would later study them. If something had to be sacrificed, it was best to let a few vertebrae go. George had to exercise his own judgment in solving this problem.

Making trenches, preparatory to removing blocks, is one of the most tedious jobs and takes the most time. The simplest procedure is to start at the face of the quarry and work toward the inside of the cliff. This means that only three sides of each block have to be channeled or cut. As a collector works, he keeps a field notebook, charting the position of the bone. George made a map on which he marked the locations of all the trenches.

Each time he exposed a bit of bone, he applied a thin layer of preservative with a small brush. Most people believe that because fossils such as these have already lasted for millions of

47

years, they are indestructible. But immediately after they are exposed to the air, they begin weathering and, if not treated, will disintegrate fairly rapidly.

Fossils may be as hard as rocks, and some are. But though hard, bones can be fragile if they are brittle. Others are soft, crumbling like charcoal. The degree of hardness depends on how they have been preserved.

Fossil-collecting tools used by paleontologists

Some have *agatized*, like the wood in the Petrified Forest and elsewhere. This means that the cells no longer remain separate and distinct but have been completely replaced with a different material. Agatized bone or wood usually appears to the eye as multicolored, frequently with reddish or red-yellow hues.

Sometimes the bone retains its original molecular structure, but the cells have been filled in with some form of mineral

A unit of bone is exposed.

matter. This process is called *mineralization* and can make the bone very hard.

Or you may find a nonmineralized bone that is preserved just as it was in life, although it may be millions of years old. Then it is hollow and very fragile — none of the pores have been filled

50

in. The material in which it was embedded has preserved it. If you remove this matrix without filling the pores in with something, the bone will go to pieces rapidly. The *Coelophysis* bones were of this sort.

The kind of preservative used depends, first, on what is available in the area where the fossil hunters are working and, secondly, on the weather conditions. George selected a very thin white shellac for use at the Ghost Ranch site. The shellacs are very good for hardening surfaces. In the field, they are almost always available from local general stores. In very damp areas, shellac cannot be used because if it is put on a wet bone, the water gets drawn up into the shellac, which then becomes milky and will not harden. George could use shellac in New Mexico because the hot, dry climate of the Southwest keeps the ground very dry most of the time, which of course means that the bones themselves are dry. Even if a slight shower comes, the hot air will evaporate the water from the ground very quickly, leaving it within a few hours as dry as it was before the rain.

If this had not been the case, George might have used one of the water-soluble preservatives such as gum arabic, which is made from resin but, in spite of that fact, can still be dissolved with water. As the specimen dries inside, this preservative will dry and harden with it.

Another water-soluble preservative is sodium silicate, commonly called water glass. This is better than gum arabic because if gum arabic gets wet again, it is likely to soften, but sodium silicate will not. Neither will shellac, for that matter. But water glass is difficult to obtain.

Alvar, another gum resin, can be used instead of shellac in dry climates. It can be diluted with either alcohol or acetone, while shellac must be diluted with alcohol. Few places in the United States sell alvar, however, since it has to be gotten from Canada. When it is available, it is preferable to shellac, having a greater penetrating and hardening ability. All in all, George preferred to use shellac.

A preservative must be thin enough to penetrate into the bone. If too thick, it will form a hard layer only on the surface, leaving the interior of the specimen soft. Then the inside is likely to dry up and begin to crumble.

In exposing the surface of the bone layer in the quarry, only a small portion of the bone was actually worked out of the matrix — just enough to determine what was inside and where each individual block could be broken off. The men wanted to utilize the surrounding rock as much as possible to help protect the bones in shipment.

Once the surface was uncovered, a very thorough coat of shellac was applied not just to the bone surface but to the entire surface of the block, paying special attention to the small cracks. These cracks sometimes come from exposure, as the block dries out after being opened up by fossil hunters. They also occur over a period of years from frost heaving. When ground freezes up, it expands and cracks. If this kind of crack occurs, it is likely to go right through the bones, breaking them. The important thing is to make the *entire* surface one unit. This means shellacking the matrix as well as the bone.

After the limits of the block have been defined and all the opened-up area thoroughly soaked with preservative, a very thin layer of Japanese rice paper is applied to the entire block with

52

LEFT, *shellac is applied to the exposed bone.* RIGHT, *applying shellac and rice paper*

shellac. This is a thin, very stringy, unprocessed absorbent paper. Processing would have removed the lint and made it look smoother and more finished in general. In Japan, rice paper is made by individual families at home and bought from them in large unprocessed sheets by manufacturers, who then either process it or sell it as is in the United States, where it is used for a number of things, including the cleaning of optical glass. When field workers don't have rice paper handy, they use facial tissues or toilet paper.

53

When the top of the block and the outer edges have been hardened with shellac and rice paper, trenches are dug around it one to two feet deep, depending on the size it is to be. This leaves the block standing by itself on a pedestal.

Next, water-wet paper is applied to the shellacked paper surface and sides of the block. Several layers are built up, and any small depressions are filled in with wads of paper so that the whole surface is relatively level. This makes it ready for the next step, plastering. The wet tissue acts as a separator between the shellacked surface and the plaster, making the "jacket" in which the block is about to be encased easier to remove back at the museum without damage to the specimen.

Trenching around the bone

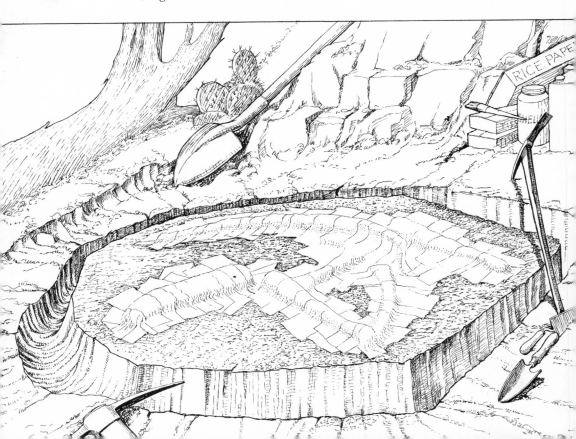

Applying wet paper on top of shellacked layer before applying plaster

With sheep shears or a knife, strips of burlap or potato sacks four inches wide are cut. These are dipped in plaster of Paris and applied in layers with the strips running in alternating directions to form what is called a "carrying jacket." The number of layers depends on the size of the block.

Next, limbs of trees or two-by-fours are used as braces. They are plastered directly to the top of the block, providing additional strength and rigidity and keeping the block from bending internally.

Now the block is ready for undercutting, so it can be removed from its position in the quarry. Using large hammers and chisels, the pedestal is reduced as much as possible by working on both sides from the face of the quarry to the back. A tunnel is then cut

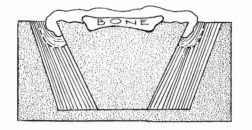

The trenches are now deepened all around the block.

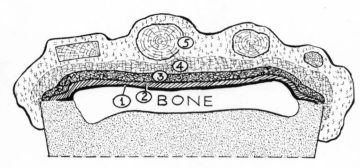

Cross-section of block:
1. shellac
2. shellac and rice paper
3. tissue, newspaper, etc.
4. burlap and plaster
5. braces of limbs or two-by-fours secured with burlap and plaster

Burlap strips dipped in plaster of Paris are applied along with braces.

Carl Sorensen undercutting the block

through the middle of the pedestal to the back, leaving the block suspended on two footings.

The next problem is to make sure the bottom of the block, between these legs, doesn't fall out. Two-by-fours, cut in convenient lengths and strapped to small cables, are put in the tunnel. Turnbuckles on top of the block are used to bring the two-by-fours up against the bottom by tightening the cables. Steel bands that come with a ratchet tightener may be used instead of the cables. These two-by-fours are then plastered into place.

A model of an undercut block

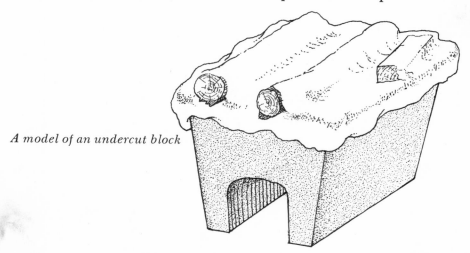

A section of the quarry face cut away to show the tunnel under the block with two-by-fours inserted

A large chain is wrapped around the entire block and attached up above to a chain block or a block and tackle. This supports it so that the legs can be removed, using large hammers and chisels. Once they are off, the block is gently rolled over. When it is lying on its top, excess rock is taken off the bottom. The same process is followed, step by step, as was done for the other side — preservative, rice paper, wet tissue, and plastering — until the entire block, top, bottom, and sides, is encased in its carrying jacket and is ready to be transported out of the quarry and back to the museum.

A model of a block with two-by-fours plastered into place at the bottom and a turnbuckle attached to the cables at the top

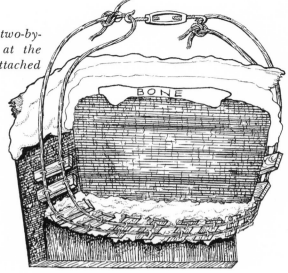

Block turned over after pedestals have been removed

The face of the quarry after the blocks have been removed

8

Throughout all this work, extensive records are kept. Back in the days when fossils were just beginning to be collected, the importance of accurate documentation was not sufficiently recognized. The variety of maps and photographs that present-day scientists use as aids was not available then, and any records kept were apt to be pretty vague. The elaborate care with which finds are now documented really began only with the present generation of paleontologists.

When this quarry was first discovered by George Whitaker, it was identified as "Ghost Ranch 2" and marked on an aerial photograph at the appropriate spot. These photographs, which can be bought from the government, cover about a square mile. They served to locate the quarry in relation to the surrounding countryside.

Quarries are also marked on area maps, or mosaics, a view drawn of a fifteen-minute, or quarter-of-a-degree, quadrangle of the earth's surface, as seen from the air. Bone that has weathered

60   *Geologic map of the Ghost Ranch area* ⟶

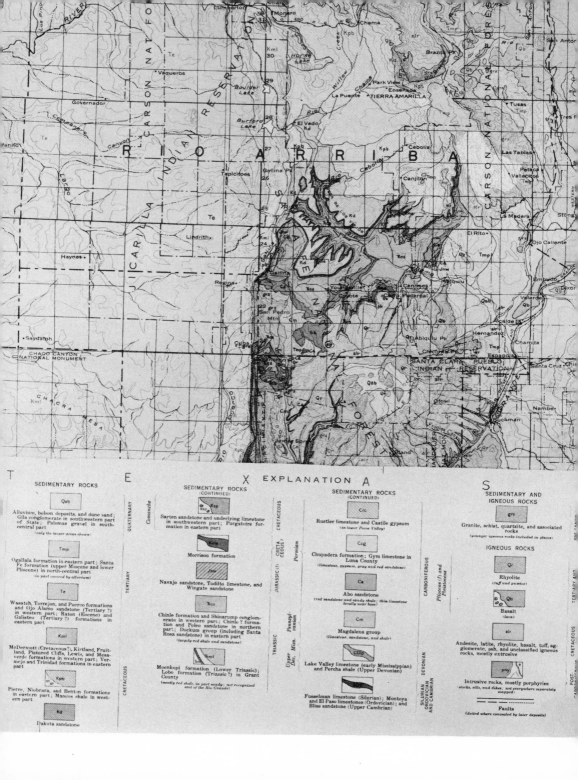

EXPLANATION

SEDIMENTARY ROCKS

QUATERNARY

Qab

Alluvium, bolson deposits, and dune sand; Gila conglomerate in southwestern part of State; Palomas gravel in south-central part
(only the larger areas shown)

TERTIARY

Tmp

Ogallala formation in eastern part; Santa Fe formation (upper Miocene and lower Pliocene) in north-central part
(in part covered by alluvium)

Te

Wasatch, Torrejon, and Puerco formations and Ojo Alamo sandstone (Tertiary?) in western part; Raton (Eocene) and Galisteo (Tertiary?) formations in eastern part

CRETACEOUS

Kml

McDermott (Cretaceous?), Kirtland, Fruitland, Pictured Cliffs, Lewis, and Mesaverde formations in western part; Vermejo and Trinidad formations in eastern part

Kpb

Pierre, Niobrara, and Benton formations in eastern part; Mancos shale in western part

Kd

Dakota sandstone

SEDIMENTARY ROCKS (CONTINUED)

CRETACEOUS — Comanche

Ksp

Sarten sandstone and underlying limestone in southwestern part; Purgatoire formation in eastern part

JURASSIC(?) — Kmr

Morrison formation

Jnw

Navajo sandstone, Todilto limestone, and Wingate sandstone

TRIASSIC — Tcs

Chinle formation and Shinarump conglomerate in western part; Chinle? formation and Poleo sandstone in northern part; Dockum group (including Santa Rosa sandstone) in eastern part
(largely red shale and sandstone)

Upper Trias. — Tml

Moenkopi formation (Lower Triassic); Lobo formation (Triassic?) in Grant County
(mostly red shale, in part sandy; not recognized east of the Rio Grande)

SEDIMENTARY ROCKS (CONTINUED)

PERMIAN

Crc

Rustler limestone and Castile gypsum
(in lower Pecos Valley)

Ccg

Chupadera formation; Gym limestone in Luna County
(limestone, gypsum, gray and red sandstone)

Ca

Abo sandstone
(red sandstone and sandy shale; thin limestone locally near base)

CARBONIFEROUS — Pennsylvanian

Cm

Magdalena group
(limestone, sandstone, and shale)

Pliocene(?) and Pleistocene — Penngl. sylvanian

MISSISSIPPIAN — CDlp

Lake Valley limestone (early Mississippian) and Percha shale (Upper Devonian)

DEVONIAN

SILURIAN, ORDOVICIAN AND CAMBRIAN

Fusselman limestone (Silurian); Montoya and El Paso limestones (Ordovician); and Bliss sandstone (Upper Cambrian)

SEDIMENTARY AND IGNEOUS ROCKS

grs

Granite, schist, quartzite, and associated rocks
(younger igneous rocks included in places)

IGNEOUS ROCKS

Qr

Rhyolite
(tuff and pumice)

Qb

Basalt
(lava)

air

Andesite, latite, rhyolite, basalt, tuff, agglomerate, ash, and unclassified igneous rocks, mostly extrusive

phy

Intrusive rocks, mostly porphyries
(stocks, sills, and dikes; not everywhere separately mapped)

————————

Faults
(dotted where concealed by later deposits)

TERTIARY AND CRETACEOUS — PRE-CAMBRIAN — POST-CRETACEOUS

out and is picked up by fossil hunters while prospecting is also marked on these maps. In case anyone wants to go back to those spots, these mosaics locate them within a few hundred yards.

The more data there are about a specimen, the more valuable the specimen becomes. In addition to the aerial maps and photographs, George and Dr. Colbert kept an elaborate system of records, varying it slightly depending upon what seemed needed at the particular locality where they were working. These records consisted of: (1) field notebooks; (2) markings on the blocks themselves; and (3) photographs.

Two pages from the Ghost Ranch notebooks are shown on page 63, drawn in the field by Dr. Colbert. They are quarry diagrams with geological remarks. A sketch of one of the skeletons, drawn by George and showing measurements and positioning in a particular block is on page 64. Although our story began in 1947, you will notice that the date of these drawings is 1948. It took two summers of field work to get the material they wanted out of the Ghost Ranch quarry.

George's notebook also contained remarks about the individual blocks, such as:

"VIII — Block taken out showing skeleton on top. It contains skull through 8″ of tail of a complete dinosaur. Animal is on right side, nicely stretched out."

and:

"IX — Contains the tail of dinosaur in block #VIII. The area of fracture between the two blocks should be opened very carefully. This block also has about 6 skulls."

These remarks, of course, coincide with or elaborate on the

62

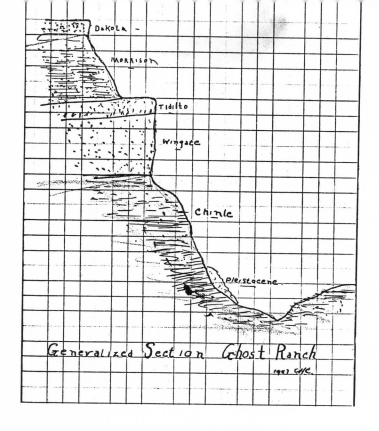

Generalized Section Ghost Ranch

Pages from Dr. Colbert's field notebook

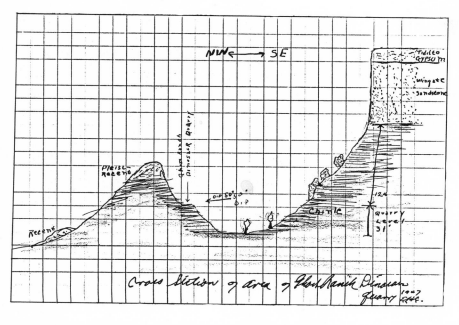

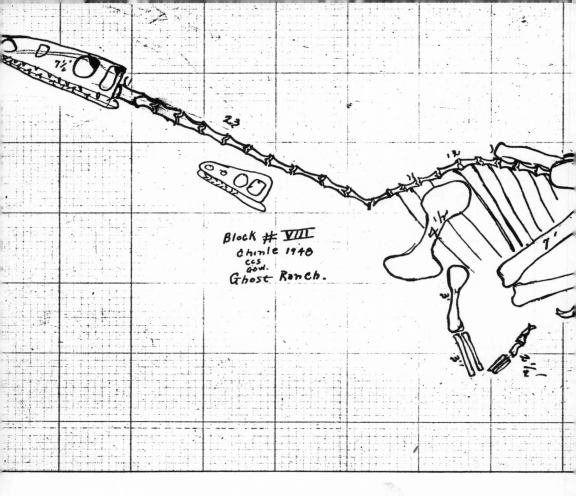

Block # VIII
chinle 1948
ccs
gov.
Ghost Ranch.

data painted on the plastered blocks themselves. Block numbers, the name of the quarry, the year of collection, and locality data are all put on at the quarry to make sure nothing gets mixed up. You can see in the photograph on page 65 how this is done. The outline painted on the block shows how the skeleton inside is resting. When the block arrives at the museum, the preparators will know, before they begin to take off the "carrying jacket," what they will find inside. This will guide them in know-

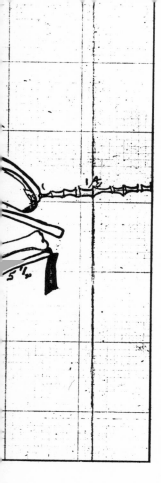

Block marked to show the position of the bone inside

A page from George Whitaker's field notebook

ing how to set about their work.

The bones themselves usually are not marked in the field, unless they have to be moved out of place. Then, if the color of the bone is light, it is labeled with black India ink. If dark, white paint is used. Or sometimes, the bones are simply packaged and the wrappings marked.

Photographs are taken at every stage — of the bones themselves, of the way the blocks are associated in the quarry, of the

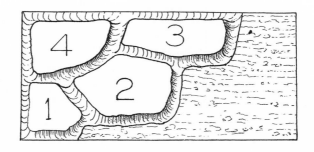

The order in which the blocks are taken from the face of the quarry is charted in field notebooks.

markings on the blocks. These photographs are placed in the field book, along with charts that diagram everything that has been done in the quarry. This means that even if some of the markings should come off, the blocks can still be matched up back at the museum. Nothing has been left unrecorded. Although it is not possible to foresee how some of these data will be used, the fossil hunter can be sure that future decisions about a quarry and the bones found there will be based on that work.

9

Braced and plastered, the Ghost Ranch blocks were enormous, weighing anywhere from 1,500 to 6,000 pounds each. Eventually there were thirteen of them. After they were marked, they were ready to be shipped back to New York, but no truck could get up to the quarry. Mr. Pack, who used to come to the diggings almost daily, asked George how in the world they were going to get the blocks off the hill.

The conversation between them went something like this.

George: "Well, we don't know. We have to do it some way, even if we have to drag them out or roll them down by hand — they just have to go."

Mr. Pack: "Well, I think the best thing for you to do is to borrow one of the big rock sleds that we have down at the ranch."

George: "You mean to tell me you have rock sleds?"

Mr. Pack said yes, that they'd been doing a lot of building and used these sleds to go up into the hills to bring out rocks to use for the foundations. The sleds would take quite a load of rocks,

67

George Whitaker at the quarry with the blocks ready for shipment

The Ghost Ranch foreman extends the road up the face of the quarry.

although they'd never hauled any as big as these plastered blocks. "I'll tell you what I'll do," he said. "I'll send my bulldozer up, and we'll snake the blocks down."

The previous road for the jeep had only come to the bottom of the hill. The bulldozer could go up the hill without a road but couldn't bring the blocks down safely. So Mr. Pack's foreman spent an entire day extending the existing road up the face of the quarry.

Until now, George had been working with a tripod made out of boards, using it to turn the blocks over in order to plaster their undersides. But the tripod couldn't lift them onto the rock sled. So Mr. Pack's foreman brought out a new tripod made of three-inch pipe.

George hitched his chain block onto it, put chains around each

George Whitaker adjusting the chain to lift the block onto the rock sled

George Whitaker lowering the block onto the rock sled

plastered block, and lifted them up with care and set them down gently on the rock sled. You can see in the picture at the top of page 71 that the bulldozer is backing down the hill. It is using its blade to steady the rock sled and prevent it from coming down too fast. When they reached the bottom, the bulldozer was turned around and hitched to the sled, which it dragged away from the quarry and down the old road to the yard of the house where the fieldmen were living. A truck had been hired to pick up the blocks there and take them to New York.

George has this passage in his field book:

"When we loaded the truck, we thought we could get it all on. But when we started, it weighed more than we thought. We put on 18,350 lbs. There were two blocks we couldn't

Carl Sorensen (in front) and Arthur Pack (on the right and wearing sun-glasses) watch the bulldozer begin to back down the hill with the blocks.

The Ghost Ranch foreman tows the blocks back to field headquarters.

get on: they are VII and XI. These were chosen as the least important of the blocks. They were out on the edge and were a little weathered. These were packed down at Ghost Ranch and left until next year for a decision about bringing them in. They were left on a sled, covered with several layers of brown tarps and some white canvas."

George returned to New York by train, while Carl Sorensen rode in the cab of the truck, keeping an eye on the precious cargo.

Once the *Coelophysis* blocks had reached New York, the Museum announced the news. The story was carried in magazines and newspapers throughout the country. It got more coverage than any other story coming out of the Museum before or since then.

On September 30, 1947, the *New York Herald Tribune* printed the following:

RICH DINOSAUR TROVE REACHES MUSEUM HERE
Natural History Officials Also Report Discovery of Big New Mexico Fossil Layer

The discovery of a new and rich deposit of mammal fossils in the clay and sandstone of New Mexico yielding significant secrets about animal life in America 60,000,000 years ago was announced yesterday at the American Museum of Natural History, Seventy-ninth Street and Central Park West.

The announcement was made simultaneously with the safe arrival at the museum from New Mexico of what is believed to be the richest collection of dinosaur and mammal fossils to be uncovered in North America. The collection was unearthed during the summer by two paleontological expeditions; one hunting early mammals and headed by Dr. George Gaylord Simpson, another looking for dinosaur remains and headed by Dr. Edwin H. Colbert.

Bill Fish and Dr. Simpson, working near Lindrith while Dr. Colbert's field party hunted the Ghost Ranch dinosaurs, had made an extraordinary find of mammal fossils. It was a memorable summer all around.

10

When the truck carrying the dinosaur blocks arrived at the American Museum of Natural History, it went directly to a basement loading platform where there is tackle built to handle just such jobs. Laboratory workers and moving men on the Museum staff gently lifted the blocks off the truck and loaded them onto rolling dollies with steel wheels.

Two of the blocks had been selected to make the exhibit that would go in the Brontosaur, or Early Dinosaur, Hall on the fourth floor. These were taken by the freight elevator up to the paleontology lab on the fifth floor. The rest of the blocks were rolled off to be stored in the basement until they could be worked on.

When the chosen blocks had reached the lab, had been taken off the dollies and set, with their undersides up, at a convenient height (above table level), a decision had to be made before work on them could begin. How were the skeletons going to be exhibited?

74

Professor Othniel C. Marsh of Yale University, one of the fathers of vertebrate paleontology in this country, felt that all fossils were too valuable to be exhibited. Instead, he had artists make papier-mâché casts of the bones and, from these, construct the models that were then exhibited in the halls at the Peabody Museum in New Haven, Connecticut.

Professor Henry Fairfield Osborn, at the American Museum of Natural History in New York City, believed people ought to see the real fossils, and his ideas are now followed by most museums throughout the world. But there are different kinds of exhibits that can be made from real fossils, and any decision depends on the condition of the bones. Lab men know, from the markings put on each block in the field, how badly crushed the skeletons inside are likely to be.

If the skeletons are fairly intact, George prefers to do a free mount, although this method of preparing a skeleton takes the greatest amount of time. It means taking the bones completely out of the matrix surrounding them and reconstructing them into a lifelike natural pose, preferably by first disarticulating all of the vertebrae.

Some years ago, most mounts were made with the animal's four feet on the ground, his backbone straight, and his head forward. Men who were doing the mounting at that time had to have the skills of a plumber because the skeletons were held up with fittings consisting of pipe with unions, t's, and joints.

Nowadays, a lab has a completely modern machine shop, including acetylene-and-oxygen welding torches and electric arc-welders. Using basic stocks of flat and half round steel, preparators attempt to fashion the metal to hold the skeletons in a lifelike pose. There is considerable art involved in keeping the frame inconspicuous. But the reconstructed animal can be made to look as if it were eating or fighting or doing any of the things it did when it was alive.

Most people do not realize how long it takes to put together the skeletons that are on exhibit. If one man worked full time without stopping, it would take him a year or two to put together a small dinosaur. The *Brontosaur* in the Dinosaur Hall of the American Museum of Natural History took fifteen years. This is not mass production work. Everything has to be done by hand. And we have already noted that it is rare to find a complete skeleton. This means that if a free mount is done, frequently some way has to be found to fill in the missing parts.

Sometimes this can be done by taking them from another skeleton of the same kind. But the preparators don't like to do this. When done, the result is always listed as a composite mount.

Sometimes, if they have one side of a skeleton, the labmen try to put a mirror image on the other side.

Preparators have found that it is best, first, to lay the animal out with the bones they have. Once everything is assembled in this fashion, it is easy to spot where pieces are missing. Then earlier collections are searched. Perhaps the men can find pieces of skeleton from another animal of the same kind. If the museum has bones that weren't collected with the new specimen, they can be used as models. The preparators make plaster-of-Paris reproductions, proportionately larger or smaller, depending on differences in the size of the two animals. These reproductions are always, purposely, slightly different in texture and color from the original bone so that they are easy to spot.

As we noted earlier, no one had ever collected a *Coelophysis* before, except for those few scraps of bone, so there was not much to compare the new specimens with. But this find had been extraordinary for the number of whole skeletons obtained, so the preparators could certainly have made up a free mount if it weren't for other factors involved.

The *Coelophysis* skeletons were birdlike. They had hollow bones, very thin and small, with a marrow cavity inside. On lightly built dinosaurs, the bone crushes readily. Where vertebrae had become squashed, it might take several years of work on one specimen to separate them. Dr. Colbert urged George to make a plaque mount of the *Coelophysis* instead of a free mount — partly because it would be faster. A complete renovation of the Dinosaur Hall was going on at this time, and exhibit space was being held for the *Coelophysis*. This sort of mount also lessened the possibility of the tiny, fragile bones being lost or damaged. And then, too, it meant that scientists could continue to study the skeleton just as it had been found.

Though George still hoped some day to make a free mount of a *Coelophysis*, that could wait for the future. After all, they had a complete herd trapped in the plastered blocks stored in the museum basement. So a plaque mount was agreed upon.

11

The preparators began work on the blocks upended in the laboratory. Excess rock had been left on the bottom of each, as added insurance against breakage or crumbling. This had to be removed, and a permanent base, strong enough to carry the weight, had to be put on.

First, the plaster-of-Paris jacket was soaked in water for several hours to soften it. Using either saws or knives or hammer and chisel, the layers of the jacket were then removed from the bottom of the block.

After all the plaster had been taken off, the rock bottom was chiseled down to a flat surface just above the bone level. Working carefully, George could see when the bones began to appear. A framework, composed of metal rods and angle irons, was welded together over this flat surface and plastered into place. This provided a sturdy, and not particularly unwieldy, base.

The block was then turned over, and the plaster jacket on top was removed in much the same manner, except that it was done with even more care. If too much of a jacket is removed at once, the plaster can pull up pieces of bone, in spite of the guard of wet tissue put between the bone and the plaster.

A nine-foot-long block would have been necessary to encompass the main skeleton George and Dr. Colbert had uncovered, and that would have been impossible to handle. So the tail of the dinosaur had been sectioned off back at the quarry in a second block. After being treated in the same way the first block had been, this was put alongside it. The two frames were then attached together to make one unit.

Delicate preparations began. Alcohol was applied with brushes to soften the shellacked surface. The rice paper, as well as the matrix surrounding the bones, had to be removed. This was accomplished by the use of straight and crooked awls, as well as a wide assortment of small dental tools. Since these were very fragile specimens, it was extremely fortunate that they had been embedded in a silt that could be dissolved by water. While the surface of the block was kept damp with either alcohol or water, little tools efficiently scraped the dinosaur bones clean. For the tiniest parts, magnifying glasses or binocular microscopes were mounted over the block. Only in a few places were small chisels used.

Two complete skeletons were exposed in deep relief. While working them out, lots of other dinosaur bones were removed from the surface, which was then covered by a coarse matrix to provide uniform background. This matrix was composed of material removed earlier from the bottom of the block and then ground up. It was authentic, therefore, having been part of the environment of these skeletons in the quarry.

George Whitaker puts the finished touches on the exhibit. (American Museum of Natural History)

While all this was going on in the laboratory, Dr. Colbert had been following the work closely. He requested an artist to make sketches, and he himself took measurements of the skeletons. His scientific studies of the *Coelophysis,* however, would not be based solely on the two dinosaurs slated for the Dinosaur Hall exhibit.

Some of the other blocks were brought up from the basement of the museum and as much bone as possible was exposed without any attempt to make it look pretty.

Based on all of this material, Dr. Colbert would then write about the probable ancestors and descendants of the *Coelophysis*. He would describe its life cycle, through his studies of skeletons in all stages of growth, from babies to adults. The measurements and drawings would give exact details of the various bones. How the animal functioned mechanically — what its muscular structure was like — would be worked out. Speculations would be made about its skin covering. To work out all possible details would take a long time.

In the meantime, the two blocks, welded into one unit with the tail matched to the rest of the skeleton so that it was impossible to tell it had been broken apart, were now ready to be put on exhibit.

The plaque mount made by the two joined blocks was extremely heavy, weighing about 1,500 pounds. It was to be supported by brackets put into the outside walls of the museum. Rods were attached to the mount, which was then slid onto the brackets so that the whole mount hung flush up against the wall. Highly skilled people from the carpentry, machine, and masonry shops in the Museum all helped with the job.

Dr. Colbert, as the scientific authority for the Dinosaur Hall, captioned the exhibit as follows:

COELOPHYSIS BAURI
Upper Triassic, Chinle
Ghost Ranch, New Mexico

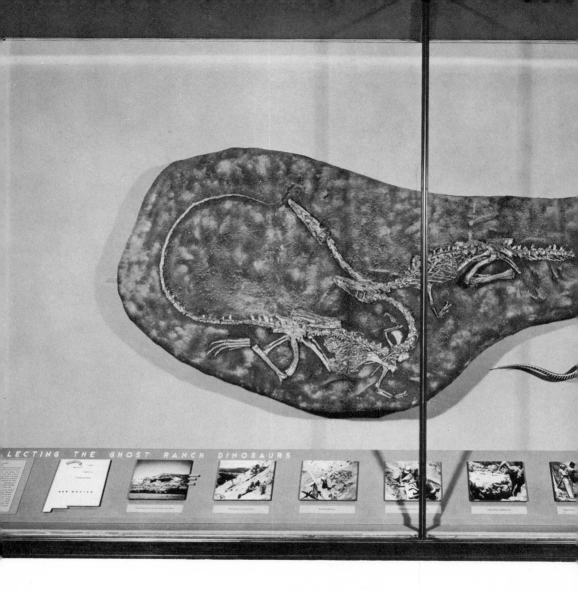

LECTING THE GHOST RANCH DINOSAURS

A brief account of the skeletons' discovery, with photographs, was put below the mount.

Some drawings, showing what the *Coelophysis* looked like,

Completed exhibit in the Dinosaur Hall at the Museum. (American Museum of Natural History)

were included in the case. One shows a skeleton upright; the other is a reconstruction of the way the animal may have looked with flesh covering its bones.

83

12

The first dinosaurs made their appearance nearly 200 million years ago. The *Coelophysis* was typical of those dinosaurs. They roamed across North America, from New Mexico to New England, in an environment ranging from lush jungles with plenty of water to arid stretches in the interior of the continent, where plants grew mostly along the streams.

Though the *Coelophysis* was a small dinosaur, it must have been ferocious. The long jaws and sharp bladelike teeth tell us it was a meat-eater. Its hind feet, strong and leaving birdlike tracks, enabled it to travel rapidly, while its front limbs, although essentially three-fingered (the fourth digit was very small), were supplied with claws that could grasp its prey efficiently.

It was a very light dinosaur, weighing no more than forty or fifty pounds, with hollow bones similar to those of birds. Standing some three feet high, it was eight to ten feet in length, down to the tip of a long tail that served as a counterbalance for the weight of its body. Most probably, its skin was leathery and flexible.

The Coelophysis *in its natural habitat*

Duckbill Dinosaurs

Horned Dinosaurs

Camptosaur Dinosaurs

Ornithischia
Dinosaurs with birdlike
pelvis

CRETACEOUS

JURASSIC

TRIASSIC

Dinosaur family tree

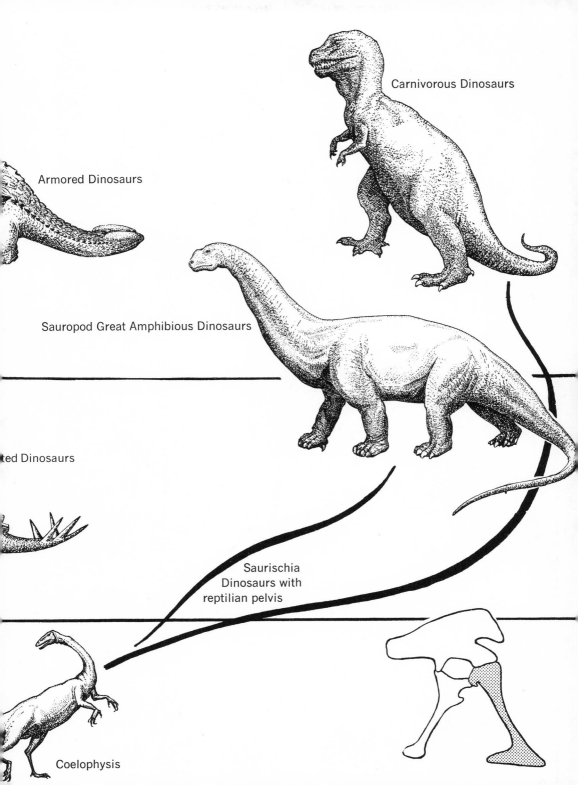

Carnivorous Dinosaurs

Armored Dinosaurs

Sauropod Great Amphibious Dinosaurs

ted Dinosaurs

Saurischia
Dinosaurs with
reptilian pelvis

Coelophysis

It may have been a cannibal, eating its own kind. Within the body cavities of the two dinosaurs on exhibit at the Museum are the remains of small *Coelophysis* skeletons. But if they were chewed, the little bones are remarkably uninjured. Perhaps the adult animal swallowed the smaller one whole.

Or it may be that the *Coelophysis*, unlike most reptiles, did not lay eggs — that these are the skeletons of babies waiting to be born. But the opening in its pelvis, through which either eggs or babies had to emerge into the outside world, is singularly small. The young dinosaurs would have had to be tiny to be born live, and the ones inside these animals are not that small. Also, their bones are unlike those of embryos, being well formed. So the best guess is that the adult *Coelophysis* did indeed eat its young.

Much of the interest that this tiny dinosaur holds is derived from the fact that, as Dr. Colbert puts it, "the basic patents" for

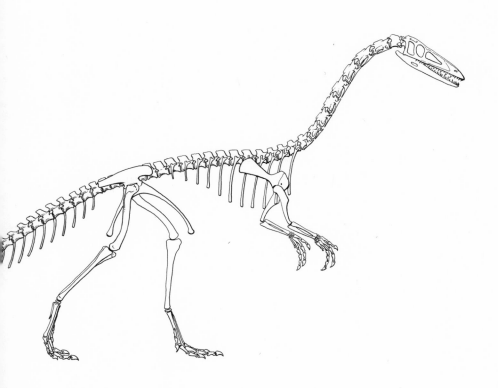

Drawing of a Coelophysis *skeleton*

the giant dinosaurs to follow in Jurassic and Cretaceous times were already there. The *Coelophysis*, though so small, was the ancestor of the more familiar giants.

The little *Coelophysis* has been reconstructed from the dead. The story of this particular dinosaur hunt ends with the installation of the small skeletons in the Dinosaur Hall at the American Museum of Natural History, But many other animals have been and will be brought back to life in much the same fashion. And each story fits into a larger one: the story of the world in which we live. Little by little, we learn more about the history of life

89

on this earth; little by little the missing gaps are filled.

"The hunter of live game is always bringing live animals nearer to death and extinction, whereas the fossil hunter is always seeking to bring extinct animals to life," wrote Henry Fairfield Osborn. He was the founder of the Department of Vertebrate Paleontology at the American Museum of Natural History. To him, as to others in the profession, there was no more honorable and fascinating pursuit than fossil hunting.

INDEX

Numbers in italics refer to illustrations.

Abiquiu, New Mexico, 19, *20*

Academy of Natural Sciences, 18

Ages of the earth. *See* Geologic timetable

Albuquerque, New Mexico, 7, 8, 10, 15, *16, 20*

American Museum of Natural History, 9, 10, 12, 40, 72, 73, 74, 75, 76, *80,* 81, *82-83,* 88, 89, 90

Articulated skeletons, definition of, 47

Baldwin, David, 18, 19, *19,* 20, 26-27, 35

Bentonite, 41, 46

Block(s)
  cross-section of, *56*
  definition of, 47
  undercut, model of, *57*
  See also Fossils

Bones, surface scraps of, 30-32, 33. *See also* Fossils

Braces, 55, *56*

Brontosaur, 74, 76

Cactus, 12, *14*

Camp, C. L., 19-20, 22

Chain block, 58, 69, *69, 70, 71*

Charts. *See* Family tree of dinosaurs; Geologic timetable; Records

Chinle, 46, 81

Climate of the Southwest, 51. *See also* Temperature changes

Coelophysis
  definition of, 10
  discovery of first bone fragments of, 18, 19, *19,* 20
  discovery of first skeletons of, 33-41
  completed American Museum

91

of Natural History exhibit
of, *82-83*

drawing of skeleton of, *88-89*

drawing of skeleton positioned
in block, *64-65*

general description of, 77, 84,
88-89

preparation of American Museum of Natural History exhibit of, 78-79, *80,* 81

representation in natural habitat, *85*

removal of fossils of, 43-59

scientific studies of, 80-81

selection of mount for, 77

skull and jaw of, *39, 85, 89*

Colbert, Edwin, 12, 15, *16,* 17,
19, 20, *28,* 30, 32, 33, 34, *36,*
37, 39, 40, 62, *63,* 73, 77, 79,
80, 81, 88

Cope, Edward Drinker, 18-19, 35

Coyote, New Mexico, *20,* 21

Cuba, New Mexico, 7, *20*

Dinosaurs

extinction of, 12-13

Triassic, 17, *18*

See also Ceolophysis; Family
tree; Identification of animal by bone comparison

Documentation. *See* Records

Ethics, paleontological, 20

Expeditions

field camps, 26, 27

field seasons, 26-27

financing of, 12

hours of work, 27-28

transportation, 26

working conditions, 28-29, 43,
45

Family tree of dinosaurs, *86-87*

Fish, William, 7, 9, 10, 12, 15, 17,
21, 73

Fossilization, types of, 48-51

Fossils

agatized, definition of, 49

definition of, 9

opening of blocks in laboratory,
78-79

preparation for removal, 37-55

removal of, 55-59, 67-72

See also Blocks; Bones

Geologic timetable, *11*

Ghost Ranch, 20, 21, *21,* 22, *22-
23,* 24, *25,* 26, 30, *31,* 43, *44,* 51,
62, 67, *68, 71,* 73, 81. *See also*
Quarry at Ghost Ranch

Hall, Herman, 43, *68, 71*

History of the earth. *See* Geologic
timetable

Identification of animal by bone
comparison, *40-41*

Ierardi, Thomas, 12, *28,* 30, 33,
34, *36,* 37, 39, *44, 46*

Jacketing
  applying, 54-55, 58
  removing, 64, 78-79
Jemez mountain range, *20*, 21

Life of the Past, quotes from, 13,
  36
Lindrith, New Mexico, 7, 10, 15,
  17, 19, *20*, 21, 30, 73

Mammals, definition of, 17
Maps
  of New Mexico, *20, 61*
  of United States, *8*
Marsh, Othniel C., 75
Matrix, definition of, 45
Meniscotherium, definition of, 17
Mineralization, definition of, 49-
  50
Mounts, different kinds of, 75-77

Natural History magazine, quote
  from, 34-35
New Mexico, maps of, *20, 61*
New York Herald Tribune, quote
  from, 72-73

O'Keeffe, Georgia, 21-22
Osborn, Henry Fairfield, 75, 90
Over-burden, 45

Pack, Arthur, 22, 24, 43, 67, 69,
  71
Paleontologist, definition of, 9-10
Peabody Museum, 75

Pedestals, 54, 55, 57, *59*
Petrified Forest, 23, 49
Phytosaurs, 19, 32, 33, 37, 39
Plastering, 54-55, *56,* 58
Preservatives
  need for, 47-48, 52
  types of, 51-52
Prospecting, 30-32, 33

Quarry at Ghost Ranch
  notebook diagrams of, *63*
  plastering face of, *44*
  platform at, *46*
  section of, *58*
  section of with blocks removed,
    59
  site of, *34, 36, 38*
  unit of exposed bone at, *50*

Records, 47, 61-66, *63, 64, 65, 66,*
  70, 72
Reptiles, definition of, 17
Rice paper, 52-53, *53,* 54, *56,* 58,
  79
Rock formations
  at Ghost Ranch, *22-23, 63*
  in Southwest, 30
  See also Over-burden
Rock sled, 67, 69, *69,* 70, *70*

Sage, 12, *13*
Shellacking, 52, *53*
Simpson, George Gaylord, 9, 10,
  13, 15, *16,* 17, 21, 36, 73

Sorensen, Carl, *25*, 40, *46, 57, 71*

Temperature changes in the Southwest, 15-16. *See also* Climate
Tools, 31, 46, *48-49*, 75, 78, 79
Trenching, 47, 54, *54, 56*

Triassic, 17, *18*, 19, 20. *See also* Geologic timetable
Tunneling, 55, 57, *58*

Undercutting, 55, 57, *57*

Yucca, *13*